MW01095076

בה

A gift from

Friends of Chabad Gala Dinner

March 16, 2017 - 18 Adar, 5777

Chabad Jewish Center
Cape Coral

MEN,
WOMEN
and
KABBALAH

Published by Jewish Innovations Info@JewishInnovations.com

Printed in China by info@pirsuminc.com   ISBN 0-9682408-3-6

By the same author:
BRINGING HEAVEN DOWN TO EARTH
BE WITHIN, STAY ABOVE
THE BOOK OF PURPOSE
HEAVEN EXPOSED

To customize for your wedding, contact info@JewishInnovations.com
Men, Women & Kabbalah is available in
a variety of sizes and formats.

MEN, WOMEN
and
KABBALAH

ancient wisdom/practical advice

compiled & translated by
RABBI TZVI FREEMAN

INTRODUCTION

First I must explain what is this thing we call Kabbalah. So I will tell you as has been said so many times before: The body of Jewishness is the deed. Kabbalah is the soul.

I cannot call it a theology, for that would imply that there is a G-d and there is a world and they are two separate entities—and this is just the notion Kabbalah comes to dispel. In Kabbalah, there is only the Infinite Light. So infinite, that even as it generates and enters a finite world, it remains just as infinite, unmoved, unchanged. Our world is only the shimmering of that light within itself. As for us, we are the rays of G-d's Mind playing among the sparks.

I cannot call it mysticism, for the mystic will tell you not to trust your eyes or any of your perceptions. But the Kabbalah is one with halacha— the legal body of Jewish thought. The great kabbalists were legalists and the great legalists were kabbalists. Halacha places its firm imprimatur on what our eyes see, our ears hear and the reality we perceive. Kabbalah teaches only to look deeper, to see the essence that connects all things, breathes life into them and regenerates them every moment from the nothingness— but never to deny the truth of our senses.

Rather, Kabbalah could be called our native cosmology, our unique way of expressing what stands beneath the surface of reality and why we do what we do.

Unique, especially because of its powerful synthesis of the outer world with the inner, of the spiritual with the practical, of the human experience with the oneness of the G-dly light. Unique in its power to accept the paradox of existence and rejoice in it.

Nowhere is this uniqueness so outstanding as in the Kabbalah of gender and marriage. Where else will you find such transcendental heights en-wrapped within the most visceral experiences of life, the deepest secrets of the cosmos unfolding into a fruitful existence on planet Earth?

In this little book, I have collected some of the most outstanding and powerful of these ideas: That gender is not just an accident, but an essential quality of the cosmos; that it is a commentary on the Divine; that intimacy is the central place of holiness without which no human being can achieve true oneness; that all the instincts planted within us are there for Divine purpose; that a true relationship is only established by reaching beyond our own egos; that in the messianic era the feminine element will rise far beyond the masculine...I will leave you to discover the rest on your own.

These ideas seem more than modern, they seem as voices from the future. Some are the diametric opposite of our standard mode of thought. Look and see: that which our culture describes with four letter words, the Kabbalah defines as the epitome of holiness! If we could transform but this one notion in our society, nothing else would remain the same.

From where does such a wisdom come? The simple meaning of the word Kabbalah will tell you: it means *received*. Kabbalah does not begin with the noisy ruminations of a human mind, but with a quietness to receive, to listen and hear the Inner Voice of the cosmos as It speaks to us, to bond with the Infinite Light and teach on Its behalf. The reception began with the first Adam, was amplified at Sinai and transmitted in an unbroken chain from enlightened teachers to their initiated students until this day.

Once we have received, then we try to understand, assisted by a wealth of metaphor and parables from our sages and teachers. Miraculously, we bring the Infinite Light into the tight boundaries of our finite minds.

When we receive much at once, the most precious jewels can fall away unnoticed. So I have collected a small but pithy selection from the masters of the Kabbalah as they dealt with the relationship of man and woman. Some provide glimpses of the depth of the inner wisdom. Some provide the practical advice that extends from that wisdom. All can be read many times and each time will uncover something new.

I have not translated literally. In many cases, that would be unintelligible. Rather, I have strived to bring the teachings of the great masters of the Kabbalah alive in our spoken language of today while preserving their voice within those words. Where necessary, I have added some elaboration, based on consonant teachings.

The responsibility is very great, for the enlightened master lives within his teachings and travels with them. I pray that they will approve of my work and that each of these lofty souls will enter your homes and marriages as you read and ponder their words from time to time. Plant them within your lives and allow them to grow and blossom.

May we all be blessed with peace between one another and between the One Above and His Shechina[1] below in an era of harmony and peace when all the world will be filled with this wisdom.

—*Tzvi Freeman, Thornhill, 5764 (2004)*

---

1   The Shechina is the Divine Presence. When we refer to G–d as transcendent, infinite and beyond, we call Him, "He". When we refer to G–d as immanently here, now, in a nurturing, inner way, we say She is the Shechina. Both are modalities of a single, simple oneness.

G-d created the Adam with His mold;

He created him to have a G-dly form;

Male and female He created them.

GENESIS 1

The initial creation of Adam was as a single body with two forms, male and female.

MIDRASH RABBA, GENESIS 8:1

*S*o the Infinite G-d looked at the Adam He had made and He said, "It is not good that the Adam is alone. I will make an equal partner[2] for him."

*N*ow the Infinite G-d had formed from the earth all the living creatures of the field and all the birds of the heavens. So He brought them to the Adam to see what he would name them. Whatever the Adam would name each living soul, that would be its name.

*T*he Adam gave names to every animal and every bird of the heaven and every creature of the field. But he could not find an equal partner for himself.

---

2   Equal partner: Literally, "a helper opposite him."

*S*o the Infinite G-d cast a deep sleep upon the Adam and as he slept, He took one of his sides and closed up the flesh beneath it. Then the Infinite G-d took that side He had taken from the Adam and built it into a woman. He then brought her to the Adam.

*T*he Adam said, "Finally there is someone who is bone of my bones and flesh of my flesh! This one shall be called Isha, because she is taken from Ish."

*T*hat is why a man abandons his father and mother and bonds with his wife and they become a single body.

*A*s they set out from their place above,

each soul is male and female as one.

Only as they descend to this world

do they part, each to its own side.

And then it is the One Above

Who unites them again.

This is His exclusive domain,

for He alone knows

which soul belongs to which

and how they must reunite.

(ZOHAR, BOOK 1: 85B)

When a person is bound in the union of male and female in a mindful way, sanctifying himself in a manner befitting this union, then he has achieved a whole and perfect oneness.

For this, a man must first ensure his wife is in a joyful frame of mind and that they both share a single will. Then their minds will be together in one place in this matter.

This way, they will be one both in soul and in body. In soul, because they bond together in a single will. In body, for together they form a single body, as we have learned: that a man who has not married is as half a person.

Now that they are whole person with a single soul and a

single body, now the One Above comes to dwell in their oneness. He emanates an aura of holiness into their union.

In this way, they have fulfilled the verse, "You shall be holy, for I, the Infinite G-d, am holy."

ZOHAR, PARSHAT KEDOSHIM

*B*egin with words that draw her heart, settle her mind and lift her spirits. This way, your mind and hers will be in one place and bond together in harmony. Speak to her of different things, some of them to awaken her desire and love, some to draw her to an awe of heaven, towards goodness and modesty. Tell her the legends of great women who merited special children through their deeds and modesty.

For if both of you will focus

your minds and hearts

towards heaven at this time,

you will be granted children whose character permits entry to spirituality and purity.

THE HOLY LETTER

There is another issue that you must give much concern, and that is to ensure that the Shechina be always with you and never part from you. Now, before a man is married, obviously the Shechina is not with him at all, since the principal element that draws the Shechina to a person is the feminine element.

In fact, each man stands between two females: The corporeal woman below to whom he must provide food, clothing and affection. And the Shechina which stands over him to bless him with all these things so that he may turn around and provide them to the woman of his covenant.

THE PALM OF DEVORAH, CHAPTER 9

The person to whom our Torah speaks is neither a man nor a woman, but both combined. For this is how Adam was first created and this is how we are in essence: Two half-bodies that are truly one. The minds are two, but the bodies, the souls and the very core of these two people are one and the same.

This is why the character and responsibilities of a man and a woman differ, for each side of the body does its part to complement the other. It would be redundant, after all, for both sides to act the same.

TAAMEI HAMITZVOT, GENESIS

When the Infinite Light emanated a world, It did so with two minds, two states of consciousness. One mind sees from above to below—and so, all is insignificant before it. From above to below, there is no world, only One.

The other mind sees from below to above—and so all of creation is G-dly to it. From below to above, there is a world—a world to point to the Oneness above.

At the nexus of these two minds, at the razor's edge of their paradox, there shines the very Essence of the Infinite Light.

The first mind descended into man; the second into woman.

That is why the man has the power to conquer and subdue, but he lacks a sense of the other.

That is why the woman feels the other. She does not conquer, she nurtures. But her light is tightly constrained and so she may become filled with harsh judgments.

As they bond together, the man sweetens the judgment of the woman and the woman teaches the man to feel the other. And in that union shines the very Essence of the Infinite.

SEFER HALIKUTIM, SHMOT, ACCORDING TO CHASSIDUS CHABAD

There are three partners in the conception of every child: the mother, the father and the One Above.

The One Above provides the breath of life. But that breath cannot enter this world unclothed.

If that breath is a new soul it is too delicate to survive here without protection.

If it has been here many times before—as with most of us—then its memory of the past, its failures and its bruises will greatly hinder it from dealing with a new body and a new life.

And so it enters with a suit, fitted for breathing life from Above while manipulating the body it is given here below.

Every thought, word and act the soul does in its lifetime must go through that suit. Even the current of blessings and life from Above must pass through its channel. The soul itself may be pure and luminous, but if its suit doesn't match, that light will have great difficulty breaking through.

How is that suit formed? It is fashioned by the thoughts and conduct of the mother and father at the time of conception. Selfish thoughts, distracted thoughts, coarse thoughts— these will provide great challenges for the child throughout life. A oneness of mind, elevated thoughts and caring thoughts—these will allow the child's soul to shine.

Even when no children are born from a relationship, there

are souls born above in higher realms. And all that a person does for those souls will return to him.

LIKUTEI TORAH, VAYERAH

*I*n G-d's mind, there are two beings, male and female, two separate forms that are one. But the physical world could not contain such a thing. In G-d's mind, two separate things can be one. In the physical realm, if they are two, they are two and not one.

Once the Adam was created as male and female in a single body and then received the breath of life, that body rose closer to the spiritual. Then the two could be separated and remain one.

This explains the strange idiom of Genesis, "a helper opposite him". "If he merits," the sages explained, "she helps him. But if he does not merit, she opposes him."

For once they have two separate bodies, by the laws of nature she should oppose him. After all, she was formed not as a child or as a parent, but as an equally important and opposite being.

But if they merit— by elevating themselves toward the spiritual— then the higher oneness of Supernal Mind will dwell between them and join them again as one.

GUR ARYEH

*I*n each of us, there is an urge to climb higher, to satisfy the yearnings of our soul. And there is another drive to indulge in pleasure, to satisfy the yearnings of the flesh. Both were planted in us by the same Creator and both are good. It is only that they must be used in very different ways.

*A*waken the yen to spiritual delight and do good deeds to satisfy it—you will awaken a flow of blessing from Above. For this desire is of the right side, which is a positive side, a side of kindness.

*A*waken, however, the impulse towards physical pleasure and satisfy your own self, this will awaken harsh judgment from Above and cause harm to the world, may G–d protect us. For this impulse extends from the left side, the side of severity and judgment. This is why anger, as well, is so harmful—as it is also of the left side and brings harsh judgment into the world, heaven forbid.

Rather, the Zohar tells us, this instinct is not created for your own sake, but for the sake of your spouse. For a man will provide a home, clothing and affection to his wife and he will do all he can to beautify her—all for the sake of this instinct. And when doing so, he will then awaken his spiritual desire and he will focus his mind and heart, saying that in this way he is beautifying the Shechina.

When he dresses her in beautiful clothes and adorns her with precious jewels, he will say, "In this way, I am enhancing the Shechina with Understanding."

So, too, when he beautifies the home, for all the

necessities of the home are for the sake of creating a dwelling for the Shechina and all the benefits his wife receives are for the glory of the Shechina.

Therefore, a man should not indulge in any pleasure except that which beautifies and benefits his wife.

This is the path we are taught in the Song of Songs, "His left hand is under my head and his right arm embraces me." First, the left impulse is awakened with passion for his wife to bond with her. And then the right hand awakens to provide for her and bring her joy in a mitzvah for the sake of a higher unity. In this way, he will sweeten all the severities and repair them with the right side.

This is the way he must deal with everything that comes from this impulse: All of it must be directed for the sake of the woman that G–d has shown to be his partner and all must then be transformed to a spiritual service, to bond in the embrace of the right hand.

SHNEI LUCHOT HABRIT,
B'ASARA MAAMAROT, MAAMAR 7

When I left my teacher to enter into marriage, I said to him, "Teacher! Bless me!"

He answered, "Sanctify yourself in the holiness of these two things, in eating and in intercourse. For all other mitzvahs do not make an impression on the body, but food sustains the body and intercourse begets the body."

IBID

MEN, WOMEN, & KABBALAH

*W*e are all matchmakers, reuniting the Shechina with Her beloved, the Holy One, blessed be He. For She is His Royalty, His word by which He creates all worlds, His breath of life that vivifies all things and makes them real.

But a schism has fallen between Her and His Infinite Light. And so He stands beyond and aloof while She dwells abandoned in darkness.

Every war upon this earth, every evil thought that plagues the human mind, all extend from this schism above. But every good deed, every fulfillment of His will here on earth, heals it. For then, He looks upon His Shechina and the earth she sustains and He sees Beauty sprouting from Her soil. Once again, He desires to dwell within Her, she rises to greet Him and His light fills all the worlds.

KESSER SHEM TOV 19, 135

*L*ook also at the last two blessings of the marriage ceremony: We first say, "He rejoices the groom and the bride"—placing the groom before the bride. But then we conclude, "He rejoices the groom with the bride." We imply that the groom's rejoicing is of secondary significance to the bride's.

*T*his is because now the bride receives from the groom, but in the time yet to come, they will be equal in their stature with a single crown as it was before the moon was diminished.

*S*o, too, we say, "Once again, in the cities of Judah and in the streets of Jerusalem, the voice of the groom and the voice of the bride will be heard." For in the future, the bride will also have a voice. The inner light of the feminine will come outward and be revealed. For then, as Solomon says in his proverbs, "A woman of valour will be the crown of her husband" — even beyond the groom.

For then, the feminine element will shine a delightful, secret light of the Hidden Mind.

Therefore, in our time, prayer is said quietly, since the bride does not yet have a voice—because presently the realm of Divine speech has no significance before the higher realms of thought and emotion, as a woman is treated as secondary to her husband.

But in the time-yet-to-come, after all is purified and healed, when the Hidden Mind of Delight and Consciousness will be revealed, then the bride will have a great voice without limit. We will say what is now the Silent Prayer in a loud voice. The sphere of Royalty—which is the sphere of womanhood— will be dominant.

*A*s the proverb goes, "A woman of valour will be the crown of her husband."

LIKUTEI TORAH, SONG OF SONGS

*T*hey are two opposites, this groom and this bride, this man and this woman. If one is water, the other is fire; one is beyond, the other within, one is achieving, the other is being—and if they are such opposites, what force can bond them as one?

True, there is love—two loves, each for the other. But even this love is of two opposite forms, bound up as it is within two opposite forms of being.

But there is a love each has which is unbounded, extending far beyond the confines of self and ego. At the point of that love, there is no distinction between them, for there they are both equally limitless beings. There, in that unbounded place of those two unbounded hearts, there they may bond as one.

So too, for the soul below to bond with her Beloved Above: The finite bonds with the Infinite, the creation with the Creator, only through the medium of unbounded love.

MEN, WOMEN, & KABBALAH

*T*he heavens kiss the earth with rays of sunlight; they awaken her with droplets of rain. Impregnated, she delivers life, she nurtures life, she sustains life.

The most spiritual heavens, the worlds of angels and souls, they do not have this power—to create being out of nothingness, to transform death into life. For the earth, in her source, is beyond the heavens. They are of G-d's light, but she extends from His very Essence. And from His Essence comes this power to cause being.

41

That is why it is the man who chases after a woman and not the other way around. For the soul of a man sees what he is lacking: the very essence, the core of being. And he sees that only in a woman can that be found.

SHAAR HAEMUNA, PG. 55

When two lips unite in a kiss, angels are born. For a kiss below is mirrored by a kiss Above where the Supernal Mind finds oneness within itself—and from this an angel is born.

But when two bodies unite as one, then souls are born. Souls that are capable of descending into this world and transforming darkness into light.

For the union of a kiss is a union of mind and heart. But in the unity of bodies, the essence of a person's being is drawn forth as a physical seed. And so, too, occurs above. For the souls are of the Essence of G-d.

How great is this mitzvah and how great the responsibility, to bring the Essence of G-d into this world!

How powerful are our thoughts and the actions that express those thoughts, for they provide the context into which that soul will descend.

DERECH MITZVOTECHA,
"THE MITZVAH TO BE FRUITFUL AND MULTIPLY"

*L*ove is best expressed by that which you do not do. Hillel the Elder said this when he summed up the entire Torah, "If you do not like something, don't do it to someone else."

What is it that you most dislike? You don't appreciate when someone pries into your faults, underlining each one with a red pen. So if you truly wish to express love to someone else, don't even look at his faults. Find whatever is good about him and talk about that.

DERECH MITZVOTECHA,
MITZVAT AHAVAT YISRAEL

s a man loves a woman,

so the One Above loves His world.

As a man desires to live with the woman he loves,

so the One Above desires to be found in all His essence within His world.

As the union of a man and woman brings children in their own image, so whenever there is oneness between creation and Creator,

between earth and heaven,

between body and soul,

between matter and spirit,

there you will find the Divine Presence

in all Her glory.

TORAT SHMUEL,
DISCOURSES FROM THE WEDDING, PG.161

"A home," wrote Solomon the Wise, "is built with wisdom."

And not with a hammer.

Because wisdom is the glue of beauty. Wisdom, meaning the ability to step back and see all of the picture. The past and, most important, the future to which all this leads. To see the truth inside each thing.

Without wisdom, there are only fragments. With wisdom, there is a whole. And there is peace between all the parts of that whole.

Not so with a hammer.

QUOTED IN SEFER HASICHOT 5704, PG. 93

*H*arsh words, demands and ultimatums—these shake the very foundations of a marriage and a home, tearing its walls apart until each one stands alone.

Gentle words, understanding words, listening words—this is the trunk from which a marriage grows, the foundation upon which a home stands.

A home cannot be repaired unless its foundation is firm. Once a couple learns to speak as friends, their marriage can endure everything, forever.

SEFER HASICHOT 5703, PAGE 233

A king without a queen, the Zohar says, is neither great nor a king. For it is the woman who empowers the man to conquer.

And it is the man who empowers the woman to penetrate and nurture.

And then the man will learn from this woman that he, too, can reach within others and provide nurture.

And the woman will learn that she, too, can conquer.

SHABBAT NOAH, 5752

*T*rue peace is not a forced truce, not a homogenization of differences, not a common ground that abandons our home territories.

True peace is the oneness that sprouts from diversity, from a panorama of colors, strokes and textures. From the harmony of many instruments each playing a unique part, not one overlapping the other's kingdom by even the breadth of a hair. There, in the most delightful beauty of this world, there shines G-d's most profound oneness.

Those who attempt to blur those borders, they are unwittingly destroying the world. Beginning with the crucial border between man and woman—for this is the beginning of all diversity, the sharpest focus of G-d's oneness, shining intensely upon His precious world.

LIKUTEI SICHOT 18, KORACH 3

*T*he relation of husband and wife is the way our world reflects the relationship of the Creator with His Creation. There is nothing more pivotal to the world's ultimate fulfillment than this.

Therefore, as the world nears closer and closer to its fulfillment, the resistance grows stronger and stronger. By now, absolutely everything appears to be undermining the most crucial key of peace between man and woman.

FROM A LETTER

Matter and energy are two opposites. To energize a piece of matter requires a constant flow.

Existence and nothingness are two opposites.

To keep the world in existence

requires a constant renewal.

Heaven and earth are two opposites.

To infuse the earthly with spirituality

requires a constant effort.

Woman and man are two opposites.

And so the marriage ceremony never ends.

LIKUTEI SICHOS, VOL. 5, P. 178

GUIDE

to a

CHASSIDIC
WEDDING

GUIDE TO A CHASSIDIC WEDDING

A marriage is a reunion of two souls. Before they descended from their holy place above, these souls were a single being. Only as they entered into a physical, human form did they become two distinct people, with two distinct personalities, traveling two different paths through life. Now those two paths have met, and those two lives must become one again.

How do we reunite two souls? With a covenant of love. Everything we do at the wedding ceremony mirrors the covenant between G-d and the Jewish People at Mount Sinai—because that is the paradigm of all covenants of love.

THE MAAMAR

Before the wedding ceremony, the groom
sits with the men while the bride sits on a
bridal throne with the women. The marriage
contract is witnessed and signed under the
supervision of the rabbi. At many weddings,
the groom then recites a *maamar*—a
deep, kabbalistic teaching concerning the
inner spiritual significance of marriage.

THE BEDEKEN

The groom has not seen his bride for at least one week. He is now escorted to her by his father and the father of the bride. As he walks, we sing. Often, the song is a wordless, meditative song composed by Rabbi Schneur Zalman of Liadi.

Upon arrival, the groom covers the face of his bride with a veil. The two fathers bless the bride. A *kohen*—a direct descendant of Aaron, the first Jewish priest—blesses her as well. The groom is then escorted away to a private room to prepare himself for the *chuppah*.

This ceremony is reminiscent of the first Jewish marriage, when Rebecca saw Isaac and veiled her face. The two are now prepared for the *chuppah* ceremony that follows.

THE CHUPPAH

In that original covenant at Mount Sinai, Moses was
responsible for arranging G-d's presence at Mount Sinai,
while Aaron, his brother, brought the Jewish People
to discover G-d there. That is why the groom comes
to the *chuppah* first, escorted by his father and the
father of the bride, and only then does the bride arrive,
escorted by her mother and her groom's mother.

The bride circles the groom seven times. In truth,
not a circle, but a spiral, rising higher and higher until
she becomes a crown on his head, as the Shabbat
is a crown to the other six days of the week.

THE MARRIAGE BLESSING

Marriage is a *mitzvah*, one of G-d's
commandments, so we say a blessing
to thank G-d for giving it to us.

This blessing belongs to the couple
themselves, but they are already in another
world, so the rabbi says it for them. They
listen carefully and drink the wine.

THE RING

Just as G-d reached out to us, to sanctify us as "a nation of priests and a holy people," so the groom sanctifies his bride by placing a ring on her index finger while reciting the words, "You are hereby sanctified to me with this ring, according to the law of Moses and Israel."

A Jewish marriage is performed by a man, a woman and two witnesses. The rabbi is here only to facilitate. The rest of us, to bring joy. The bride is absorbed in silence and stillness. The groom is transformed by doing, she by quietly being.

THE MARRIAGE CONTRACT

Now we now read the *ketuvah*, the original marriage contract, composed for the protection and security of the bride. It states the principal obligations of the groom to provide food, clothing and affection along with other contractual obligations. It is written in Aramaic, since that is the most precise language for these sorts of legal documents.

Once read, the rabbi hands the *ketuvah* to the groom, who presents it to his bride.

If the *ketuvah* is lost, the couple cannot live together until a new one is written. Because marriage is not a one-time event, but a continual process of caring and providing.

FULFILLMENT

The second half of the *chuppah* ceremony begins when we say a series of seven blessings. We bless them that they will discover that same delight in one another that they knew in their pristine, primal state.

The marriage between G-d and the Jewish people that began at Mount Sinai is not consummated until the messianic era when the world will be "filled with divine wisdom as the waters fill the ocean." Since that time has not yet arrived, the *chuppah* ends with the groom smashing a glass, representing the shattered state of our world, awaiting our repair. The crowd exclaims, "Mazel Tov!" with joy, hugs and tears.

The bride and groom are then escorted to a private room where they must be alone for a few minutes. A small snack awaits them there, since they have been fasting all day.

The souls of the groom and the bride now reunite to become one soul, as they were before they entered this world. We share in their joy with boundless dancing and singing.